Coloring For Fun
« Ocean Underwater Life »
25 Coloring Pages Of Ocean Underwater Life…

Aline Boosks
LanicartBooks.com

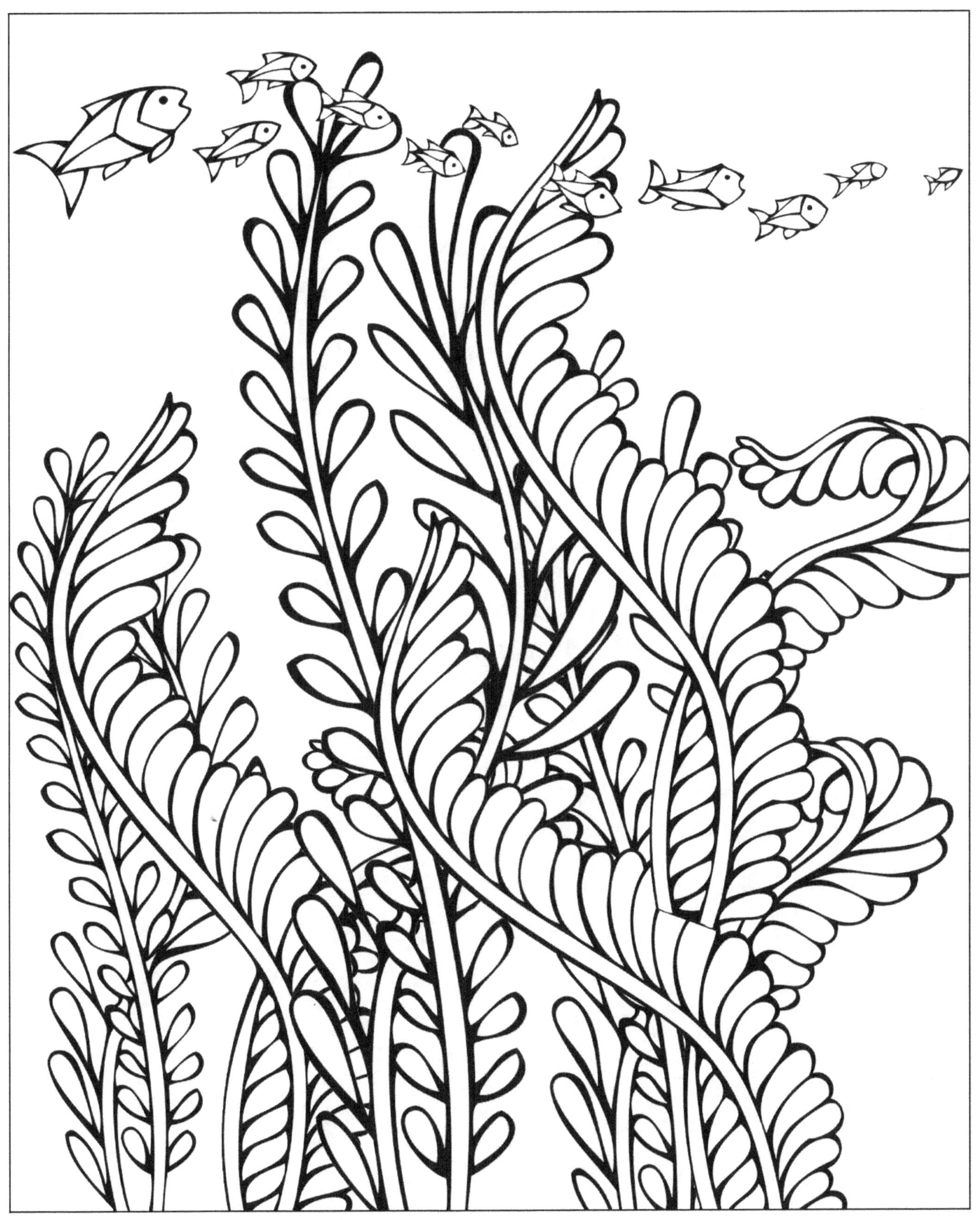

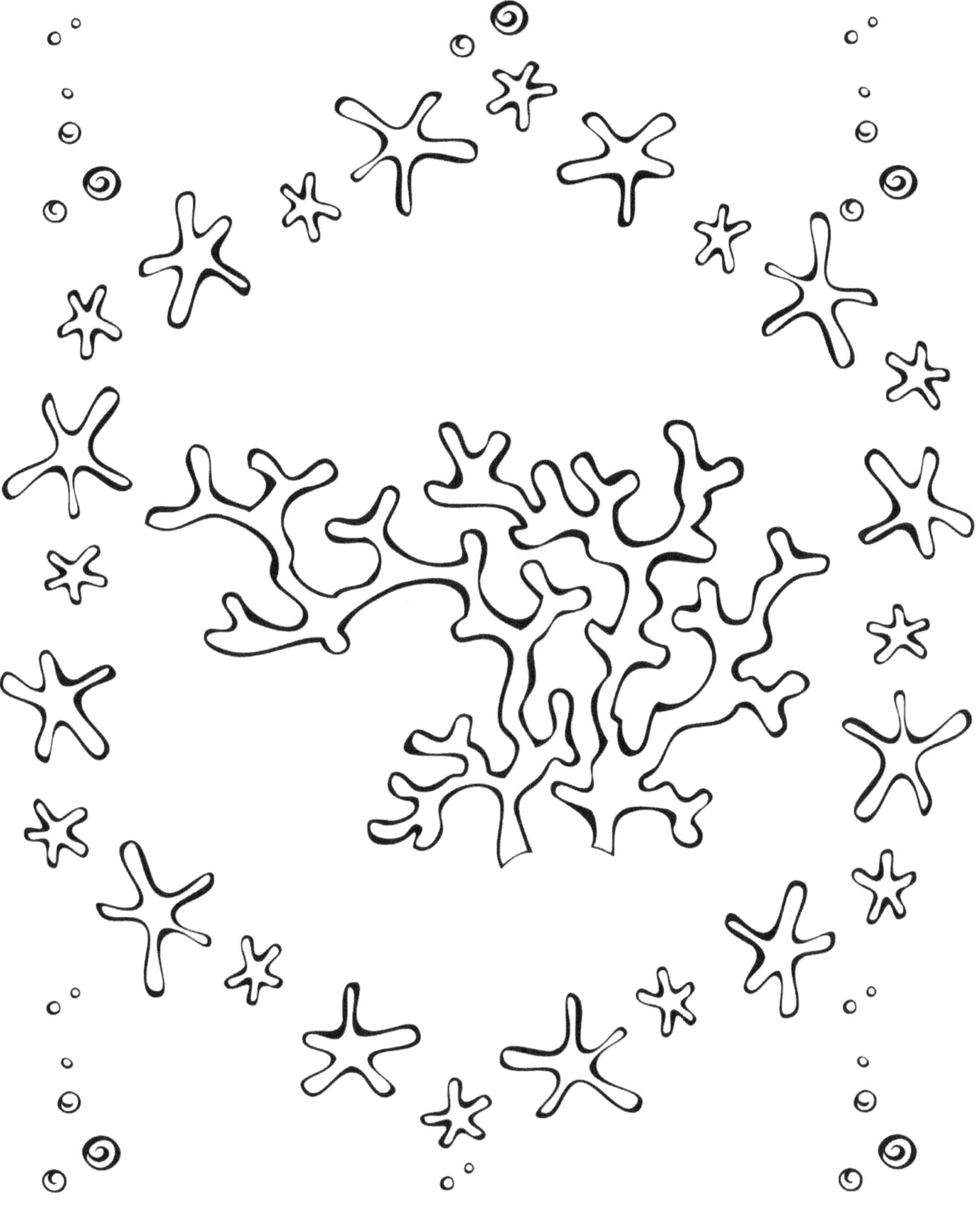

www.ingramcontent.com/pod-product-compliance
Lightning Source LLC
Chambersburg PA
CBHW081601270726
48657CB00029B/3463